Albert
the Running Bear's
Exercise
Book

Albert
the Running Bear's
Exercise Book

by Barbara Isenberg & Marjorie Jaffe
Illustrated by Diane de Groat

CLARION BOOKS
TICKNOR & FIELDS: A HOUGHTON MIFFLIN COMPANY
NEW YORK

Note: Exercise can be stressful and must be performed in the exact manner prescribed in this book. The authors and the publisher shall have no liability, personal or otherwise, for any consequences resulting from the procedures herein.

Clarion Books
Ticknor & Fields, a Houghton Mifflin Company
Copyright © 1984 by North American Bear Co., Inc.

Printed in the U.S.A.

Library of Congress Cataloging in Publication Data
Isenberg, Barbara.
Albert the running bear's exercise book.
Summary: A friend convinces Albert he can
become a better runner by doing additional
exercises. Outlines an exercise program with various
levels of difficulty.
1. Exercise for children—Juvenile literature.
2. Aerobic exercises—Juvenile literature. [1. Exercise]
I. Jaffe, Marjorie.   II. de Groat, Diane, ill.   III. Title.
RJ133.I84   1984   613.7'1   84-7064
RNF ISBN 0-89919-294-7
PAP ISBN 0-89919-318-8

P 10 9 8 7 6 5 4 3 2 1

To our children, Christopher, Bryce, and Ian,
who helped us test the exercises,
and to Amanda, who helped us test the huggability of Albert.

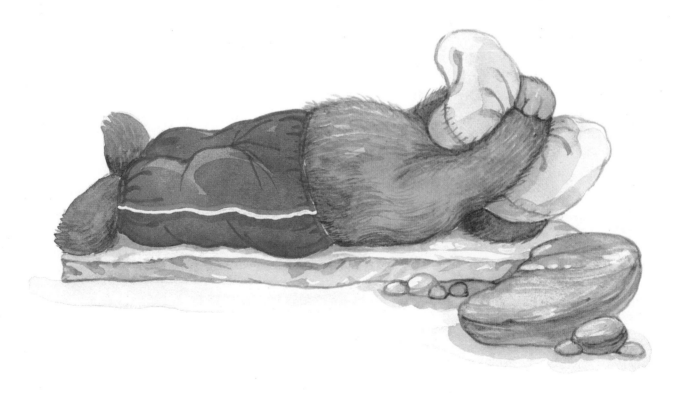

A Note to Parents and Teachers

The exercises that Albert the Running Bear learns in this book are geared to children between the ages of five and nine.

Exercise is important for children because it makes them more aware of their bodies through a sense of muscle balance, correct alignment, and increased limberness. If properly performed, exercise not only will help children to look and feel better, but can become a healthful habit that will serve them all their lives.

Marjorie Jaffe, co-author of the book, has conducted exercise classes for both adults and children. She is a trained exercise therapist, taught by Dr. Sonya Weber, co-founder of Columbia-Presbyterian Medical Center's Posture and Back Care Clinic in New York City. For ten years Ms. Jaffe was head of the Y.W.C.A.'s back-care program in New York, and she is the author of an exercise book for adults, *Get Your Back in Shape.*

In this book Ms. Jaffe provides a large variety of exercises, but it is not necessary to do them all at one time. Children can pick and choose the ones they like best or feel most comfortable with and still get a great deal of good from them. For instance, the Animal Jamboree of aerobic exercises is fun and beneficial even if done by itself.

The directions should be followed exactly so that the exercises will be effective and safe. It is best if an adult supervises the first few sessions, to make sure that the children understand the directions and are not doing anything to hurt themselves or make them feel uncomfortable. If a child has a medical problem, a doctor should be consulted before he or she does any of the exercises.

The Authors

P.S. Even a creaky, nonexercising adult might benefit from this book by exercising with a child!

Contents

1. Albert Meets Violet

Early one fall morning, Albert the Running Bear was awakened by loud thuds coming from the next cage.

"Who's there?" Albert wondered. "That cage was empty yesterday." He shuffled sleepily to the bars and poked his snout through to investigate. There before his eyes was the most beautiful bear he had ever seen. And she was moving around in a strange way.

"Ahem," said Albert, clearing his throat loudly.

But the new bear did not look up.

"Maybe some of my old circus tricks will get her attention," thought Albert, so he began to whistle a tune and waltz around his cage.

She still did not look his way.

Albert picked up the fish from his food bowl and began his juggling act. When he missed his timing and the fish landed smack on his head, he heard a little giggle.

At last Albert had the bear's eye. "Hi," he said. "Who are you—and what are you doing?"

"I'm Violet," she answered shyly as she stretched her body from side to side. "And I am exercising."

"Why?" asked Albert.

"I need to keep my muscles in shape in case I ever go back."

Albert didn't want to be too nosy but he couldn't help asking, "Go back where?"

"To show business," Violet answered as she bobbed up and down, touching her toes.

Albert's eyes widened. "Are you a movie star?"

"No," said Violet, grabbing hold of her heel and stretching her leg straight up in the air. "I was trained as a gymnast and a stunt bear. But when it came time to perform in front of people, I got scared and ran off."

Violet finally stopped moving and gave a long, sad sigh. "My trainer heard about a retired circus bear who lives here, and thought he might be able to help me. This bear is now a famous runner. But I'm sure he wouldn't want to meet a scaredy-cat like me." Violet hung her head.

Albert pointed to himself proudly with both thumbs. "You're talking about me, Albert the Running Bear, and don't worry—I'm pleased to meet you. Maybe you could teach me some of your exercises."

Violet looked surprised. "Don't you know any exercises, Albert? I thought all runners and athletes exercised."

Albert was embarrassed that he didn't know any, so he decided to make one up.

"Sure, I know some exercises," he said. "What do you think of this one?

"Wiggle your ears,
Snuffle your nose,
Twiddle your thumbs,
And shuffle your toes."

Violet giggled. "That's very funny, Albert, but it doesn't really get you moving."

"Then how about this one?" said Albert.

"Shake your belly,
Then jump all around,
Twirl five times,
And fall on the ground."

"That's got a lot of action," Violet said, "but not the kind that makes you stronger."

"All right, I have an idea," said Albert. "Why don't you teach me some real exercises, and I'll try to help you get over your stage fright."

"It's a deal," said Violet. They clasped paws on their bargain and decided to start that day.

Keeper Norman, who had been watching his two special bears, was glad to see that they had become friends. He opened the door between their cages.

2. Finding Out What Albert (and You) Can Do

"First I'll give you a few tests to see what shape you're in, Albert."

"You don't need to do that," said Albert. "Feel my muscles. They are hard and strong from running."

"But some muscles shouldn't be hard, Albert. Muscles always work in pairs. When one is tight and hard, its opposite needs to be loose and stretched."

Albert was puzzled. "Why should any muscles be loose?"

"So that you can bend and reach and move easily," answered Violet. "Other muscles need to be tight and firm to help you work and play hard."

Test Number One:

Hamstring Muscles

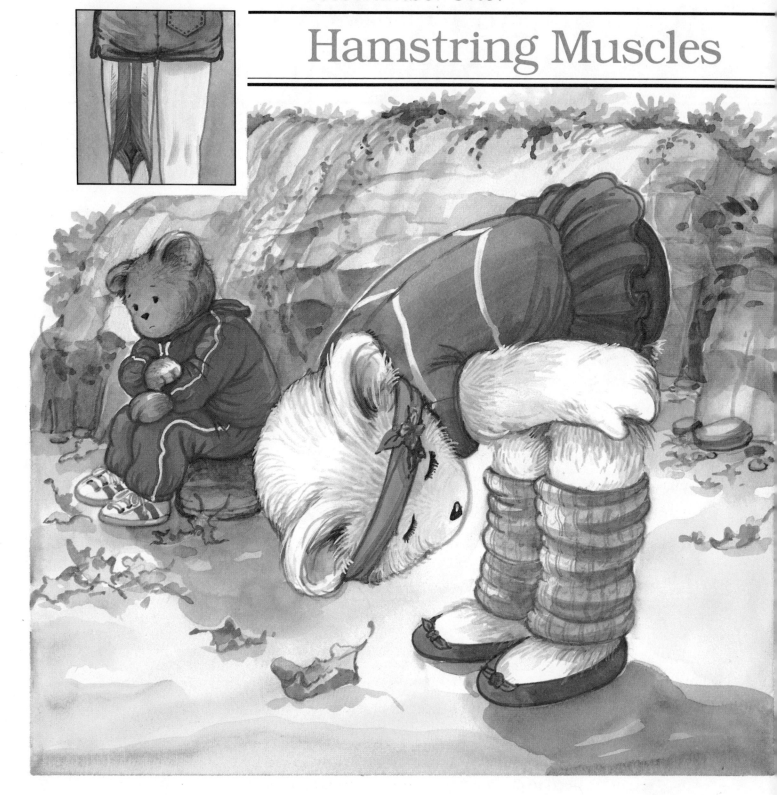

"Can I take the tests, now?" asked Albert. He was eager to begin because he was sure he was in perfect shape.

"All right, Albert. First we'll see how flexible your hamstrings are. These are the long muscles on the back of your thighs. If your hamstring muscles are too tight, you'll feel a sharp pull when you bend over."

Violet told Albert to stand with his knees straight and his belly pulled in. "Now," she said, "drop your head, bend over and see if you can touch your toes."

Albert chuckled. "That's easy. Anyone can do that." He bent down to try, but his fingers dangled four inches above the floor, and he could feel a sharp pull behind his knees.

"You have firm quadricep muscles on the front of your thighs from running," Violet said. "But all runners need loose hamstrings, too. Otherwise your legs will ache after you run."

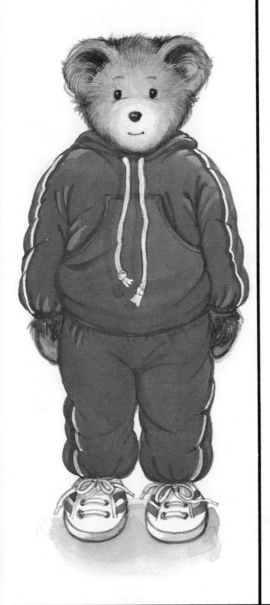
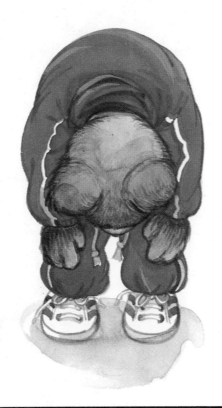

See if you can touch your toes. If you can't, have someone measure the space between the floor and your fingers. Then as you do the exercise over and over, you can measure your improvement.

Pectoral Muscles

"Now, let's see how stretched your pectoral muscles are," said Violet. "These muscles start at the tip of your shoulders, fan out across your chest, and tie on to each rib."

Albert caved in with laughter as Violet outlined the pectoral muscles on his chest. He was a very ticklish bear!

Violet waited for him to get his giggles under control and then continued. "If your pectoral muscles are too tight, they pull your shoulders forward and you look hunched."

Violet told Albert to stand about eight inches from the wall. "Now," she said, "stretch both arms upward, palms facing each other, and try to touch the wall behind you. You must keep your arms straight and not arch your back."

"This will be a cinch," thought Albert, raising his arms. A look of surprise came over his face when he could not reach the wall. His head poked forward and his back arched.

Violet patted Albert on the back and smiled. "These opposite muscles are very strong," she said. "They are called the rhomboid muscles, and they hold your shoulder blades in place."

Try this test and see if you can touch the wall. Remember, don't arch or lean back.

21

Test Number Three:
Abdominal Muscles

"Do I have to take any other tests?" Albert asked. He was beginning to wonder if he was in such good shape after all.

"There's just one more," said Violet. "It's for your abdominal muscles."

"Abdo...what muscles?"

"The ab–dom–i–nals," repeated Violet slowly. "These are the muscles on your stomach. The rectus muscle runs up and down your belly. The four oblique muscles crisscross it. And the transverse muscles go across your waist and tie up your whole belly."

Violet started to outline these muscles on Albert's stomach, but stopped when she remembered how ticklish he was.

"My stomach muscles are nice and loose already," said Albert, grabbing hold of a hunk of fur and fat. "I'm sure I can pass this test!"

"I'm afraid not, Albert," said Violet. "This time you need just the opposite. You should have firm, tight abdominal muscles to support your back, so that you can stand up straight and tall."

Violet pointed to the ground and asked Albert to lie down. "Now," she said, "I'm going to hold your feet and you put your paws behind your head.

"When I count to three," said Violet, "lift your head, pull your belly in and roll up. One, two, three."

After much struggling, Albert managed to sit up. But he was discouraged. He grabbed a handful of jelly beans from his pocket to cheer himself up.

"Do you really want those, Albert?" Violet asked. "It'll be lunchtime soon."

Albert looked down at his belly, and then he put the rest of the jelly beans back in his pocket. He didn't want Violet to think he had no willpower.

Have someone hold your feet and you try a sit-up, too.

3. Getting Ready to Exercise

After lunch, Violet ran to her trunk and brought out a picture of the back with lots of wiggly lines on it. "Those lines are your nerves," she explained to Albert. "They hurt if your muscles press on them. This could happen if your posture is poor or your abdominal muscles are too weak to hold up your body.

"Stand up and let's look in my mirror," Violet said. Albert saw a curve in his lower back that looked big enough for a banana to fit into it.

"We'll have to work on that, Albert," Violet said. She pulled out another piece of paper from her trunk and walked to the wall. "I'm going to pin up this chart so you can see how you should look."

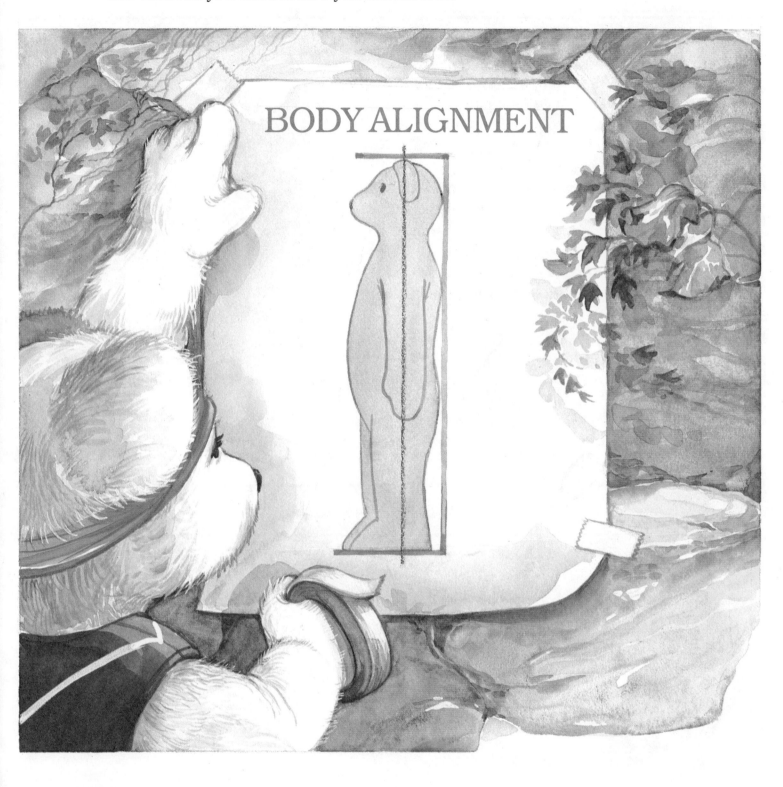

BODY ALIGNMENT

Try to stand correctly yourself. Is your body lined up like the one on the chart?

Breathing

"Are there many more tests?" Albert asked. He was starting to get a bit fidgety. "I'd like to go for a run."

"No, we'll soon be through for today," said Violet. "But I do want to show you how to breathe."

"I know how to breathe," said Albert. "If I didn't, I wouldn't be alive, would I?"

"I mean deep breathing. You need lots of oxygen for exercising properly. When I say *inhale* I want you to breathe in through your nose slowly and raise your ribs. Let's sit down and try."

Albert inhaled and his chest blew up like a bullfrog's.

"*Exhale,*" continued Violet, "means to breathe out slowly through your mouth and lower your ribs. If you make a hissing sound when you exhale, you can hear all the air come out."

Albert tried this. He liked having the air come out in a long, loud hiss, and made an even louder noise the second time.

Try inhaling and exhaling slowly.

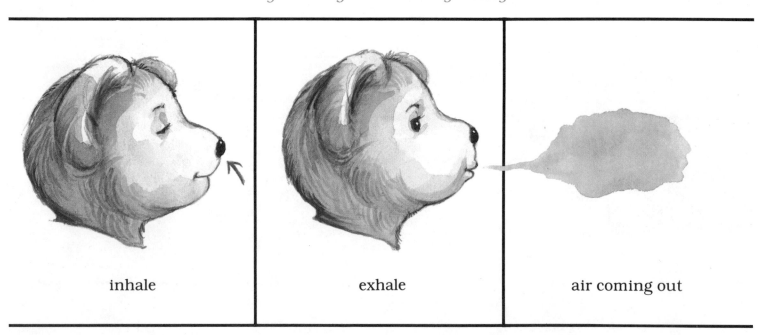

| inhale | exhale | air coming out |

"Good," said Violet. "Next I'll show you how to work your feet." She stretched her legs straight out. "During some of the exercises we do I'll tell you to flex or point your feet."

Flex and Point

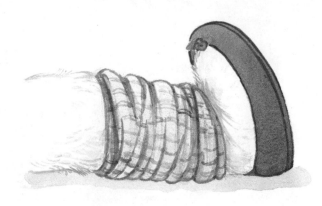

"**Flex** means to pull your toes toward you and stretch your heels away."

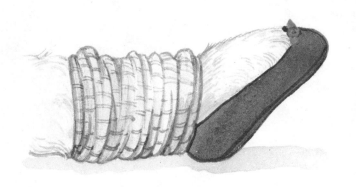

"**Point** means to stretch your toes down."
   Albert tried flexing and pointing his toes a few times. It was easy and it felt good.

Now you try flexing and pointing your toes.

   "That's it for now," said Violet. "Have a good run, Albert, and I'll see you tomorrow. I'd like to start very early before the crowds come. I couldn't exercise if anyone was watching."
   "That's fine with me," said Albert. "I'm an early riser." He pulled himself very straight and walked slowly back to his cage to ring for Keeper Norman. As he went, he took long, deep breaths.

Albert got up very early the next morning and rummaged through his locker. At last he found what he was looking for—one of his old circus costumes. He was sure it would impress Violet.

First he put on his tight tuxedo pants and then his purple shirt, bow tie, and sparkly sequined jacket. Next he pulled on his high black leather boots. Finally he tapped his top hat in place and strutted into Violet's cage.

"Ta-dum!" Albert sang out as he entered the cage.

"Why, Albert," said Violet, "you look sensational. Are you going to a party?"

"No, I've come for my exercise class. Don't you remember?"

"Of course I remember, Albert, but you won't be able to exercise in that lovely costume. You need to wear clothing that you can move easily in. Go and change back into your running suit. Bring your sleeping mat with you, too."

It's always best to wear comfortable clothing like shorts or sweat clothes for exercising. When you have to lie down, you can use a blanket on a carpeted floor, a mat on a bare floor, or a grassy spot outside.

4. The Exercises

Albert returned in his running suit, dragging his sleeping mat behind him. While he was gone, Violet had posted a list of rules next to the body chart. She told Albert to take a look at them.

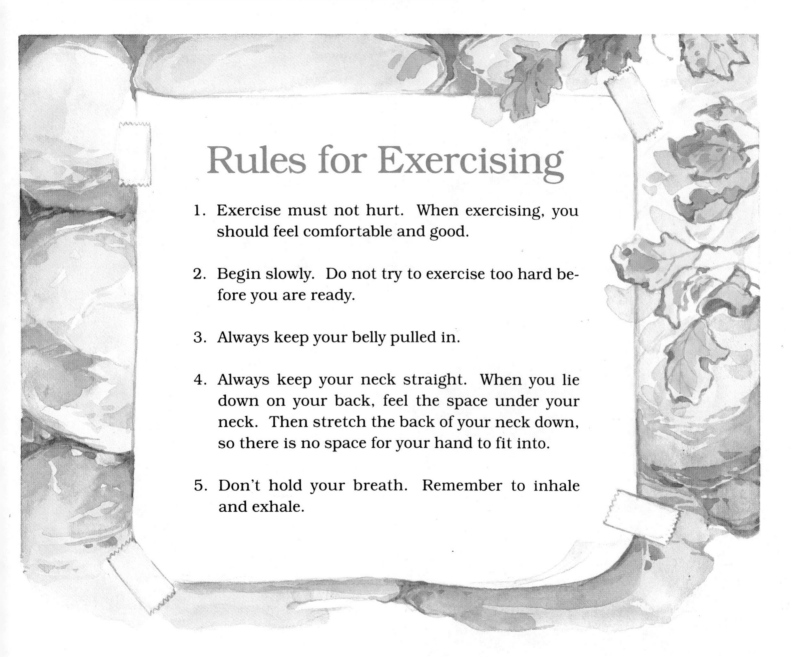

Rules for Exercising

1. Exercise must not hurt. When exercising, you should feel comfortable and good.

2. Begin slowly. Do not try to exercise too hard before you are ready.

3. Always keep your belly pulled in.

4. Always keep your neck straight. When you lie down on your back, feel the space under your neck. Then stretch the back of your neck down, so there is no space for your hand to fit into.

5. Don't hold your breath. Remember to inhale and exhale.

Read this list of rules each time before you start to exercise. Soon they will become automatic.

Super Stretch

"Now we're ready to begin, Albert," said Violet. "The first exercise is called the Super Stretch. It'll help to get you as stretched and straight as possible."

	**1.** Lie on your back, arms down, legs down, and feet flexed.
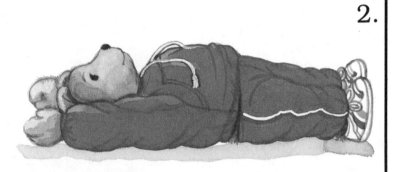	**2.** Inhale and stretch your arms up. Then exhale, but keep stretching.
	**3.** Drop one arm down at a time and feel your body loosen.

Try the Super Stretch yourself and repeat the exercise five times.

Knee Bumps

"That felt good," said Albert.

"Next we'll do an exercise to stretch your hamstrings and tighten your abdominal muscles," said Violet.

1. Lie on your back, arms down, knees bent.

2. Lift your head and right knee. Keep your belly pressed in. Then bump your forehead and knee together.

3. Lower your head and right knee to the floor. Then do the same exercise with your head and left knee.

Do these Knee Bumps and repeat the exercise three times. Don't bump too hard!

Hamstring Stretch

"That wasn't so hard, Violet."
"Good. Now I'll give you another exercise to lengthen your hamstrings," Violet said.

1. Lie on your back, arms down, left knee bent, and right leg straight.

2. Flex your right foot and raise your right leg, keeping it straight. Then hug your right leg and press it gently toward you.

3. Bend your right knee. Then lower your left foot to the ground, and repeat the whole exercise with your left leg.

When you do this Hamstring Stretch yourself, you should repeat the whole exercise three times.

Rock and Roll

"Do you know any way to relax?" asked Albert. "I feel a little sore."

"This next exercise will help you to relax. It'll also stretch your lower back," said Violet.

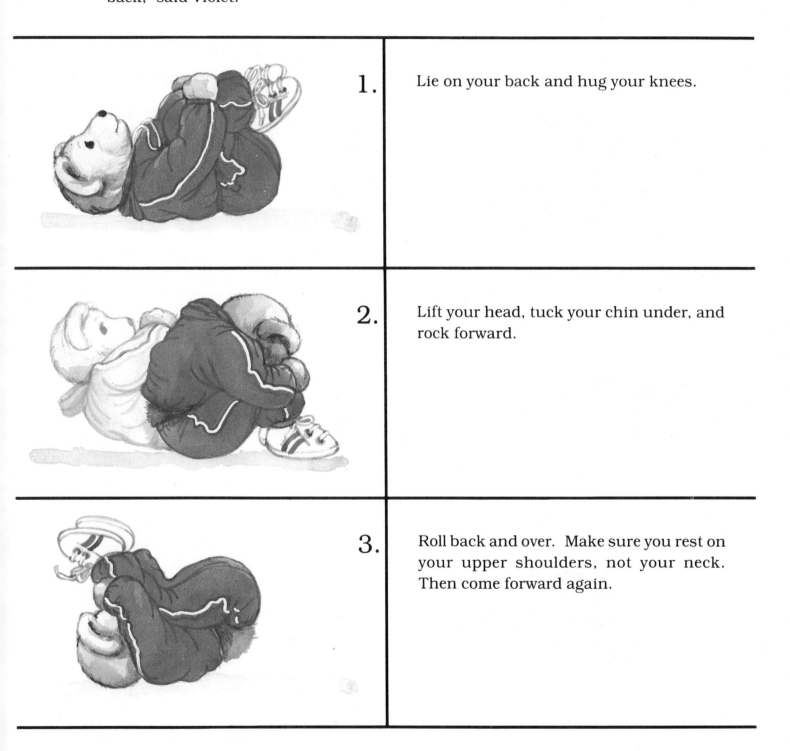

1. Lie on your back and hug your knees.

2. Lift your head, tuck your chin under, and rock forward.

3. Roll back and over. Make sure you rest on your upper shoulders, not your neck. Then come forward again.

Try the Rock and Roll yourself and repeat the exercise five times.

Curl Backs

"Now, Albert," said Violet, "stay forward when you come back from your last Rock and Roll, and we'll do an exercise for your abdominal muscles."

1.

LEVEL 1

Sit with your knees apart and your arms down. Keep your feet on the floor.

2.

Roll down. Stop just before your waist touches the floor and say three times:

Jelly belly go away,
Hard, strong tummy's here to stay.

3.

Squeeze your belly in hard, inhale, and roll forward.

Repeat the whole exercise five times. Move on to Level 2 when you feel stronger. Then move on to Level 3.

LEVEL 2

Fold your arms on your chest, keep your feet on the floor, and follow steps 2 and 3 above.

LEVEL 3

Put your hands behind your neck, plant your feet firmly on the floor, and follow steps 2 and 3 again.

"Phew," said Albert, after trying Level 3. "It's hard to curl back and keep my feet down, too."

"I know," said Violet, "but you'll get stronger." She smiled. "Now are you ready for another stomach tightener?"

Albert gave a little groan.

Sit-ups

1.

LEVEL 1

Lie on your back with legs straight. Point your feet and keep them down. The arms are overhead.

2.

Lift your head, keep your chin down, and swing your arms up to a sitting position. Press in your belly tightly!

3.

Pull your head and shoulders forward. Keep your belly in and your knees slightly bent. Reach forward to stretch your hamstrings.

4.

Roll slowly back into the floor with arms at your sides and your belly in tight.

Follow the directions carefully so that you can do the Sit-ups safely. Make sure you tighten your stomach muscles rather than your back muscles. If the straight-leg sit-up is uncomfortable, try the bent-knee position

LEVEL 2

With arms at your sides, repeat Level 1 directions.

LEVEL 3

With arms folded across chest, repeat Level 1 directions.

LEVEL 4

With hands behind neck and elbows back, repeat Level 1 directions.

LEVEL 5

With knees bent, start with Level 1 positions and increase up to Level 4 position. This is harder to do than straight-leg sit-ups, but sometimes it is more comfortable. Whatever level you do, you must always keep your feet down.

(see Level 5) with someone holding your feet.

When you can do the first level comfortably ten times, then move on to the next level, and then the next.

Wing Circles and Flings

"Those were *really* hard," said Albert, after trying all four levels.
"Don't worry," said Violet. "If you do some every day, they'll soon seem easier. Now let's try a gentle stretching exercise for your pectoral muscles."

1. Sit cross-legged with your arms stretched out to the sides, palms up.

2. Make ten big circles as far back as you can, then drop your arms, wiggle, and relax.

3. With your arms out and the palms up again, squeeze your shoulder blades together. Fling your arms back ten times, then drop your arms and relax.

You can do Wing Circles and Flings, too. It's best to do ten of each.

Round Back–Flat Back

"This next exercise will stretch your back muscles," said Violet.

1. Start on your hands and knees. Keep your belly pulled in.

2. Drop your head and make your back round like a frightened cat's.

3. Lift your tailbone and flatten your back like a table.

Try the Round Back–Flat Back and repeat the exercise five times.

Runner's Reach

"That was fun," said Albert.

"Good," said Violet. "I'll give you another stretch that you'll really enjoy. It's called the Runner's Reach, and it'll stretch your calf muscles."

1. Start on your hands and knees with your toes tucked under.

2. Lift your tailbone, stretch your legs straight back, lean forward, and raise your heels.

3. Lean back and try to press both heels down. You'll feel your hamstrings stretching.

Try the Runner's Reach yourself. You can do it with both heels down or one heel down at a time. Either way, you should repeat the exercise five times.

Leap Frogs

"Will the Runner's Reach help my running?" Albert asked.

"It should," said Violet. "The Runner's Reach and the Hamstring Stretches loosen your leg muscles so they won't hurt or get stiff after you run. Now I'll give you an exercise for the quadricep muscle on the front of your thighs."

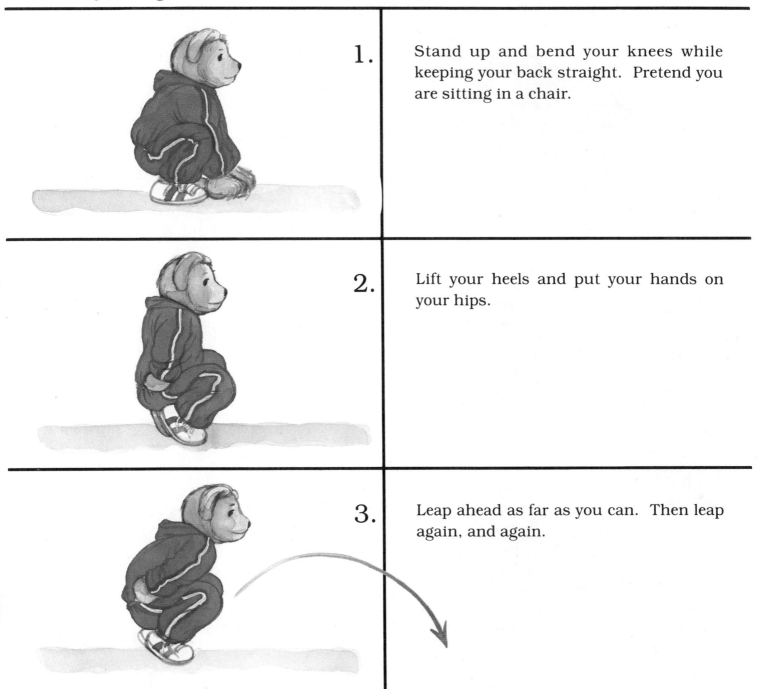

1. Stand up and bend your knees while keeping your back straight. Pretend you are sitting in a chair.

2. Lift your heels and put your hands on your hips.

3. Leap ahead as far as you can. Then leap again, and again.

You can leap forward or backward or in a circle. Leap until you run out of breath!

Push-ups

Albert could leap for a long time, even though he huffed and puffed a little. "I really felt my leg muscles working," he said.

"Let's do an exercise to strengthen your arm muscles now," said Violet.

1.

LEVEL 1

Lean forward on your hands and knees, and rest on your thighs.

2.

Bend your arms, lean forward, and touch your forehead to the floor. Don't let your belly touch the floor.

3.

Straighten your arms and move back to the starting position.

Repeat this exercise five times at first and then work up to ten times. When you can do ten Push-ups comfortably, move on to Level 2. It's hard, so don't get discouraged.

1.

LEVEL 2

Lean forward on your hands and toes, with your legs straight, and your tailbone up in the air. Then follow steps 2 and 3 as before.

2.

Bend your arms, lean forward, and touch your forehead to the floor. Don't let your belly touch the floor.

3.

Straighten your arms and move back to the starting position.

Try to work up to ten Push-ups on Level 2. Then you'll really be good!

Cat Stretch

Even though Albert's arms were very strong, he could only do five push-ups on the first try. He went on to Level 2, but couldn't do it comfortably. "Remember the rules, Albert," Violet said. *"Exercises must not hurt* and you must *begin slowly.* Let's end today's class with a good stretch."

1. Sit on your heels and round yourself over, arms straight.

2. Lift your tailbone and keep it perfectly still above your knees.

3. Slide your chest and arms forward and bounce gently while "meowing" like a cat. Then return to the starting position.

Do the Cat Stretch five times. Let yourself really relax and stretch forward as far as you can. But always keep your tailbone above your knees, the way Albert is doing.

5. The Animal Jamboree
(Aerobic Exercises)

Albert and Violet did their exercise routine every morning that week. Albert began to feel comfortable, and he especially enjoyed the exercises that made him feel like another animal. He was just finishing a Cat Stretch when suddenly he jumped up.

"What is it, Albert? Did you hurt yourself?"

"No," he said, "I just had an idea. Wouldn't it be great if all of the animals in the zoo could exercise together?"

"What a good idea!" said Violet. "We could have a jamboree and do aerobic exercising."

"Do what?" asked Albert.

"Aerobics are exercises like running and hopping that make your heart pump faster and better," explained Violet.

The next morning, Albert told Julia, the giraffe in the next cage, about the jamboree. He asked her to pass the word along to the other animals. In no time at all, a loud cheer went up and the animals started running and jumping and hopping and flapping around in their cages.

Keeper Norman rushed out in his pajamas to see what the ruckus was all about.

"Uh-oh," said Albert.

But Norman wasn't angry. He was pleased when he realized that his animals were just trying to get some exercise, so he decided to let them all out onto Albert's track.

Albert took Violet by the paw and went to the center of the track to explain what she had taught him about aerobics. Violet blushed at the mention of her name, but became less shy when Albert asked her to help demonstrate the jamboree exercises. He led the way with the first one.

Maybe you would like to join the jamboree, too, or have your own jamboree with some friends. Start by repeating the rhyme for each exercise two times. As your stamina increases, repeat each exercise for a longer period of time. The ultimate goal is to do the jamboree for twenty minutes without stopping. But don't push it . . . it takes a while. Practice each animal's movement before you begin.

Albert's Run

Run in place. Run fast until you're tired, then run slowly. Try to run with your knees high and then low. Go only as fast as you can breathe easily, but keep on going and repeat:

Keep it moving, keep it moving,
Run along with me.
Keep it moving, keep it moving,
Join the jamboree.

Next, Albert asked one of the chimpanzees, who was jumping up and down, to come forward and make up an exercise. All of the animals followed what the chimpanzee did.

The Chimp's Tap

Jump in place and clap your hands in front a few times to start. Then bend your right leg back and tap your right hand to your heel. Jump and clap in front again, and then repeat the exercise with your left leg and left hand. Keep jumping and changing sides from right to left. As you jump, you can say this rhyme:

Keep it moving, keep it moving,
I'm a chimpanzee.
Keep it moving, keep it moving,
Join the jamboree.

51

The elephant could hardly wait for her turn. She waddled out into the middle of the track and swung her trunk wildly to show everyone her exercise.

Elephant Trunk Swings

Slow down but keep running in place. Lean forward and clasp your hands together in front of you to look like a trunk. Kick your heels back as you shift your weight from foot to foot and swing your "trunk." At the same time repeat:

Keep it moving, keep it moving,
Swing along with me.
Keep it moving, keep it moving,
Join the jamboree.

The kangaroo hopped out next. Everyone enjoyed doing her jumping exercise.

Kangaroo Jumps

Take four jumps forward and four jumps backward. Next, try four jumps to the left and four jumps to the right. Now try to do two jumps in each direction and then one jump in each direction. (This will be harder. Just remember, kangaroos have been doing it longer than you!)

Use this counting rhythm for your jumps instead of the regular one:

Jump, two, three, four,
Back, two, three, four,
Right, two, three, four,
Left, two, three, four. <u>Then:</u>
Jump two, back two, right two,
  left two. <u>Then:</u>
Jump, back, right, left.
Jump, back, right, left.

When everyone finished jumping, Julia the giraffe came forward. She decided to do some head rolls. They were especially good for her long neck.

Giraffe Rolls

Stand with your legs wide apart, keep your arms at your sides, and let your body sway gently from side to side. Roll your head around *very* slowly in big circles to exercise your neck. Make four circles in one direction, then four circles in the other direction.

Keep it moving, keep it moving,
Roll along with me.
Keep it moving, keep it moving,
Join the jamboree.

The crane flapped out to the middle of the track. He wanted to have a try, too.

Crane Flaps

Stand with your feet together and your arms at your sides. Then jump your feet apart, flap your arms up overhead, and clap them. Without stopping, return to your starting position. Repeat as many times as you can. If you need a rest, use only your legs and leave your arms at your sides.

Keep it moving, keep it moving,
Flap along with me.
Keep it moving, keep it moving,
Join the jamboree.

The animals tried not to laugh when the hippopotamus got up to take her turn, but she looked so funny rolling her hips.

Hippo Bumps

Stand with your legs apart and your hands on your waist. Make four circles with your hips, first in one direction, then in the other direction.

Keep it moving, keep it moving,
Bump along with me.
Keep it moving, keep it moving,
Join the jamboree.

The camel showed them a nice, easy exercise to do with their feet because they were all beginning to get tired.

Camel Walk

Stand straight with your feet slightly apart, arms at your sides. Raise up the heel on your right foot and keep your other foot flat. Lean forward onto the ball of your right foot. Then bring your right foot back down and raise the heel of your other foot. Keep shifting your weight from foot to foot and say:

Keep it moving, keep it moving,
Clop along with me.
Keep it moving, keep it moving,
Join the jamboree.

The armadillo wanted to lead the last exercise. He walked very, very slowly to the center of the track, stood there for a moment, and then curled himself into a ball. It was the only exercise the armadillo could do, but it made a perfect ending to the jamboree. All of the animals curled into balls as best they could, closed their eyes, and relaxed for a while.

Armadillo Curl

Put your knees on the floor and sit on your heels. Drop your head and shoulders down to the floor and curl yourself into a ball, just like the armadillo.

While the animals were relaxing in the armadillo position, a clear voice was heard from the center of the track. "Keep your eyes closed and get up slowly," the voice said. "Stand with your legs apart and drop your head and shoulders down toward the floor. Wiggle your whole body from side to side and feel your muscles stretch and loosen. Continue to wiggle and slowly stand up."

When they all opened their eyes, there was Violet, leading the exercise. The animals cheered and thanked her for the jamboree. Violet made a graceful curtsy in response.

After they got back to their cages, Albert smiled at Violet and said, "I think our bargain has worked."

"What do you mean?"

"Well, I'm running better than ever, and you were terrific just now when you led the last exercise."

Violet gasped. "Why, you're right, Albert! I forgot about my stage fright. I wasn't scared at all."

Soon word got out that the zoo animals were exercising, and crowds of people came to watch. But Violet didn't mind. She was happy to be showing others something useful. And besides, she didn't have to perform by herself anymore. She had her friend and partner, Albert, by her side.